THE COLLABORATIVE ARTIST

Three Characters

by RANDALL FABER

VIOLIN

VIOLA

PIANO

This work was commissioned by Music Teachers National Association to feature and promote collaborative music. It was premiered at the MTNA Conference on April 3, 2016, San Antonio, Texas.

FABER
PIANO ADVENTURES®

Performance Notes

A listener may presume the Three Characters to be portrayed by the three instruments of the trio. Instead, the characters manifest in the unfolding sections of the work, ultimately depicting three aspects of the human persona: serenity, emotion and action. The simplicity of the opening develops with hint of a plaintive call. The middle section settles in rhythmically to present emotional reaching to the divine and the divine reaching down. The final section, a chromatic fugue, weaves an unrelenting twelve-tone subject with the plaintive theme in a forward drive of raucous activity.

ISBN 978-1-61677-199-7

Three Characters

for piano, violin, viola

Randall Faber
(b. 1954)

Three Characters
for piano, violin, viola

Viola

Randall Faber
(b. 1954)

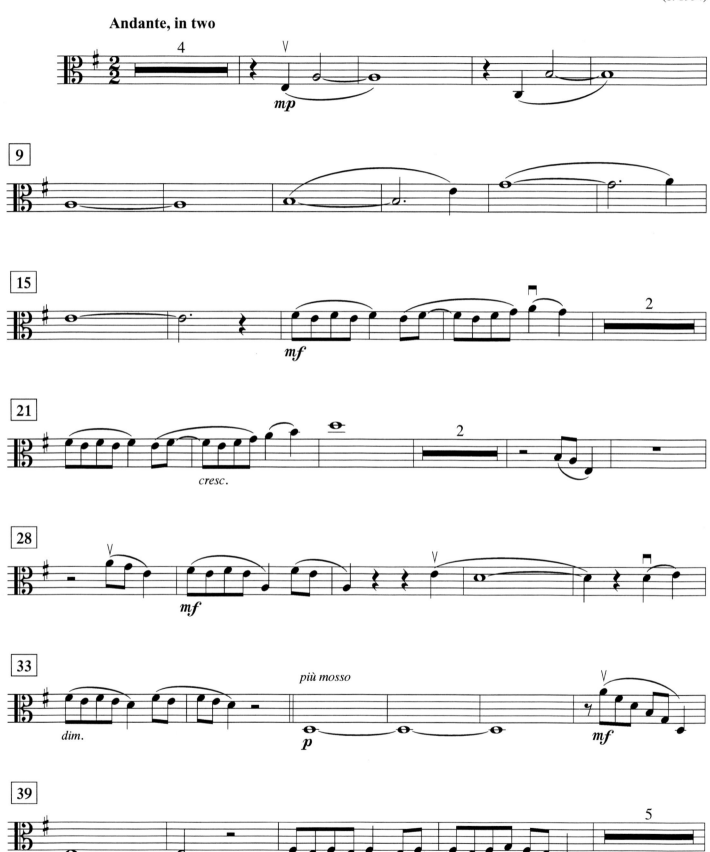

Viola

FF7009-Viola

Three Characters
for piano, violin, viola

Violin

Randall Faber
(b. 1954)

Andante, in two

Violin

-2-

Violin

FF7009-Violin